THE FIRE WITHIN
WHEN PURPOSE MEETS BUREAUCRACY

DR. DARRYL S. DIGGS, JR.

Copyright 2025 Achievementfourall LLC - All rights reserved.

The content contained within this book may not be reproduced, duplicated or transmitted without direct written permission from the author or the publisher.

Legal Notice:
This book is copyright protected, It is only for personal use. You cannot amend, distribute, sell, use, quote or paraphrase any part, or the content within this book, without the consent of the author or publisher.

Disclaimer Notice:
Please note the information contained within this document is for educational and entertainment purpose only. All effort has been executed to present accurate, up to date, reliable, complete information. No warranties of any kind are declared or implied. Readers acknowledge that the author is not engaged in the rendering of legal, financial, medical or professional advice. The content within this book has been derived from various sources. Please consult a licensed professional before attempting any techniques outlined in this book.

Published by AchievementfourALL LLC
Paperback ISBN: 979-8-9858167-5-4

Acknowledgments

This book would not have been possible without the bravery of those who choose to fight not only the fires in front of them but also the slow-burning fires within their own organizations. To every firefighter, every paramedic, and every first responder who has ever felt the weight of bureaucracy stifle their purpose, your stories are the heart of this book.

To leaders who are committed to understanding the reality on the ground and who have the courage to ask the difficult questions, you are the architects of a better system. We acknowledge those who are actively working to tear down silos, create stronger lines of communication, and build a culture where competence and purpose are valued above all else. Your efforts to connect people to their mission and to one another are the truest form of leadership.

A special thanks to the brave individuals who speak up, even when it's uncomfortable, and to those who support them. Your commitment to transparency and truth is what lights the way for change.

Finally, to all those who refuse to let the fire within be extinguished by the chain that binds, this book is for you. You are the spark.

The Fire Within: **A Bureaucratic Burn**

A Satirical Guide to Organizational Dysfunction
Dr. Darryl S. Diggs, Jr.

ONE

Chapter 1: The Meeting About Meetings

"Listen up, we have to do this," Chief Thompson announced, using his favorite phrase—the same words he'd used to introduce every pointless initiative for the past five years.

Captain Sarah Martinez watched her firefighters draw stick figures on whiteboards, unknowingly creating the most accurate organizational chart the department had ever seen.

The fire chief is drawn as a tiny stick figure with a huge hat. What are the key lessons here about the relationship between perceived authority and actual competence?

Chapter 2: The Translation Game

Jake drew a fire truck surrounded by speech bubbles: *"We show up to save lives, but first we wonder if we'll get written up for using too much water because someone in accounting thinks water is expensive."*

It was like playing telephone, except the message started as "save lives" and ended as "submit Form 47-B for hydrant usage approval."

What is the most effective way to communicate a lack of clear purpose to a large group of people while also making it sound incredibly urgent and mission-critical?

Chapter 3: The GPS That Doesn't GPS

Maria sketched herself looking terrified—not of fire, but of addresses. *"If it's in the rich neighborhood, we better have our act together. Poor neighborhood? Response time isn't tracked as carefully there."*

Apparently, GPS systems work better when property values are higher. Who knew technology was so economically conscious?

Write a mission statement for a new technology company that promises to "untrack" response times for low-value zip codes, ensuring an equitable distribution of delayed services.

Chapter 4: The Chief's Communication Strategy

Chief Thompson had perfected the art of creating communication barriers. His favorite technique? The "information hoarding huddle"—where important decisions were made in his office with the door closed, then filtered through six layers of management until they emerged as completely different instructions.

"Transparency is overrated," he often said. *"Confusion builds character."*

The chief believes "confusion builds character" and "transparency is overrated". Develop a three-step plan to "manage mediocrity" by hoarding information and filtering it through six layers of management.

Chapter 5: The Trickle-Down Theory

The Chief's decision-making process was like a game of bureaucratic telephone mixed with broken plumbing. Information would start at the top, then leak, spill, and evaporate as it traveled down until frontline workers received something completely unrecognizable.

"I decided you'll all work overtime on Sundays" became *"Someone might need to do something on weekends, possibly."*

What is the ideal amount of "leaking, spilling, and evaporating" for information to be completely unrecognizable by the time it reaches the frontline?

The chain of command has become a "chain that binds". How can you leverage this binding effect to prevent your employees from actually doing their jobs?

Chapter 6: The Equity Task Force (RIP)

The Diversity and Equity Task Force had lasted exactly three months—long enough to identify real problems, short enough to be disbanded before anyone had to actually fix them.

"We don't need a task force to tell us we treat everyone equally badly," Chief Thompson explained when he dissolved the group.

The Equity Task Force lasted only long enough to identify problems before being disbanded. What is the optimal lifespan for a task force so that it appears productive without ever actually fixing anything?

Write a eulogy for a good idea that was killed by "colorblind leadership," ensuring you praise the idea's "potential" while celebrating its swift and painless demise.

If we "treat everyone equally badly," does that count as a successful equity initiative?

Chapter 7: The Budget Meeting Reality

"We need to cut costs," announced Finance Director Patricia Chen, spreading spreadsheets across the table like battle plans. "Fire trucks are expensive. Have you considered using smaller vehicles?"

Captain Martinez stared at the woman who'd never seen a structure fire. "Smaller vehicles can't carry enough water or equipment to—"

"But the cost-per-mile efficiency would improve dramatically," Chen interrupted, highlighting numbers that meant nothing when someone's house was burning.

What are the five most important spreadsheets a finance director should create to ensure that the mission of the organization is completely lost in a sea of data?

Chapter 8: The Community Voice

Mrs. Rodriguez had lived on Elm Street for thirty years. She'd watched response times get longer as the neighborhood got poorer.

"When my grandson called about the apartment fire, he timed it," she told the city council. "Fourteen minutes. Same fire in Hillcrest would get a four-minute response."

She held up her phone with the recording. "This isn't about procedures. This is about who matters."

The room went quiet. Data is easy to dismiss. Human voices aren't.

The book states that "data is easy to dismiss" but "human voices aren't". How can we, as bureaucrats, find a way to dismiss the human voices by either turning them into irrelevant data points or just ignoring them completely?

Draft a prepared statement for the city council, acknowledging Mrs. Rodriguez's "passion" while promising to form a committee to "study the feasibility of potentially addressing" the issue of response times.

Chapter 9: The Union Perspective

Union Rep Tony Castellanos had seen chiefs come and go. "Every new administration promises change," he said. "Then they realize change is hard, expensive, and makes people angry."

"So we protect our people by following procedures exactly. You want us to risk our necks because some consultant thinks they know better?"

He had a point. Bad systems create defensive behavior. Fix the system, and you might fix the behavior.

Tony Castellanos argues that bad systems create defensive behavior. To what extent are complex procedure manuals and union contracts not just about safety, but about creating a protective barrier against the organization's own incompetence?

When is it more beneficial for an organization to maintain an "unfixable" system than to simply fix the behavior?

Chapter 10: The Credential Collectors

Deputy Chief Wilson had never fought a fire, but he had three degrees in Public Administration and a certificate in "Synergistic Leadership Excellence." He was often seen managing crises by forming committees to discuss the possibility of maybe addressing issues.

His management style could be described as "confident incompetence."

DEPUTY CHIEF WILSON

You are Deputy Chief Wilson. Draft a memo proposing a new committee to address a non-existent problem. Include at least three new bureaucratic euphemisms for "doing nothing" in your proposal.

What's the secret to "confident incompetence," and can it be taught in a seminar?

Chapter 11: The Nose That Knows Nothing

Assistant Chief Martinez (not to be confused with Captain Sarah Martinez) had a PhD in Organizational Psychology and zero understanding of actual organization. She spent most of her time eavesdropping on conversations she didn't understand, then making policy based on fragments she'd overheard.

Her specialty was being exactly wrong at precisely the right volume.

What is the most effective way to be "exactly wrong at precisely the right volume"?

Is it possible to get a PhD in a field and have "zero understanding" of it, or is that the point of a PhD in organizational psychology?

Chapter 12: The Manual That Manuals

"The manual tells us what we can't do," Sarah observed, *"but it never asks what we should do."*

The 847-page Standard Operating Procedures manual had a section on proper paperclip usage but nothing about saving lives efficiently. Priorities were clearly established.

Why is it more important to have a manual that tells you "what you can't do" than one that asks "what you should do"?

If common sense is the foundation of a house built from a manual, what happens when you remove that foundation?

Chapter 13: The Water Wars

Tom drew himself giving a hose to a child, then crossed it out. Every community interaction now required approval from Legal, Risk Management, Community Relations, Public Affairs, Budget Office, and the Committee for Preventing Good Ideas.

"By the time we get clearance, the school year's over," he muttered.

Develop a new approval process for community interactions. Your plan must include at least seven different departments, including the "Committee for Preventing Good Ideas".

By the time a community interaction gets approval, the school year is over. How can we slow down the approval process even further to ensure that no good ideas ever get off the ground?

Chapter 14: Resume Rich, Decision Poor

The people making policies had impressive CVs and zero practical experience. They'd never run into a burning building, never told a parent their child didn't make it out, but they sure knew how to write reports that sounded good to city council.

"MBA: Making Bad Assumptions," Maria added to her whiteboard section.

The "Equipment Decision Committee" requires "no experience" to join. What are the three most important qualifications for a committee that makes decisions about equipment they will never use?

You have an impressive resume and zero practical experience. Draft a report that uses lots of corporate buzzwords to explain why you have just decided to buy a bunch of worthless equipment.

Chapter 15: The Real Cost Counter

Jake started keeping a different kind of log:

"March 3rd: Delayed 6 minutes for equipment inspection that could have been done during downtime. House fire spread to garage."

"March 8th: GPS rerouted through construction zone. Added 4 minutes. Patient transported by family member instead."

"March 15th: Chief required supervisor approval for mutual aid. Neighboring city's faster response saved two lives we couldn't reach in time."

Every bureaucratic barrier had a human cost. Some costs just weren't measured.

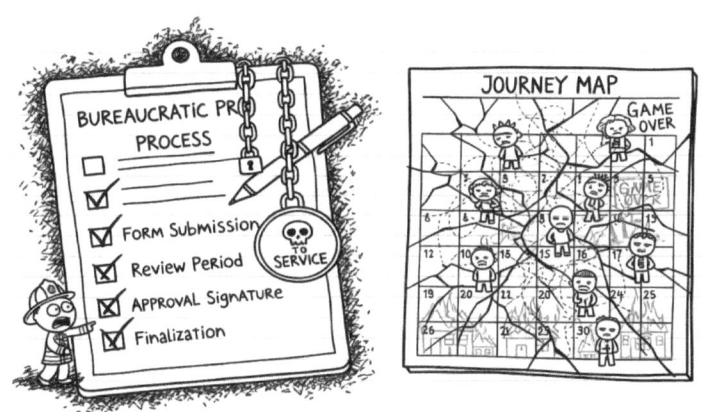

The "Bureaucratic Process" is a secure, chained-up checklist. What is the optimal number of checkmarks on a bureaucratic process checklist to ensure that the mission of the organization is "Game Over"?

What's the key to making a "journey map" look like it has been through a war zone, and what are the benefits of a "game over" outcome?

THE BUREAUCRATIC SLOW-BURN: A CONTROLLED ORGANIZATIONAL BLAZE

1. What is the most absurd example of bureaucracy presented in this section, and why is it so damaging?

2. How does the "Real Cost Counter" challenge the traditional understanding of efficiency and metrics?

3. Why do the characters, like Jake, initially feel powerless against the bureaucratic system?

4. Can you identify a real-world parallel to "The Meeting About Meetings" in an organization you know?

5. How does the narrative arc of Act One build a sense of mounting frustration for the reader?

6. Discuss the difference between a "rule" and a "purpose." How does this act show that a system focused on rules can lose its purpose?

7. What kind of "fire" is Jake logging, and why is it more dangerous than the physical fires they are meant to fight?

TWO

Chapter 16: The Spark That Started It All

Maria didn't ask permission. When the call came about the apartment fire on Elm Street—the same neighborhood where response times "varied"—she made a decision that would light a fire under the entire system.

"Sarah, I'm two blocks away. Going in."

Sometimes the most radical act is simply doing your job.

Maria's radical act is "simply doing your job". What does it say about an organization when the most radical act is performing the function the organization was created for?

If a hero saves a life, but they didn't get an "Approval Signature" first, did they really save a life?

Chapter 17: The Hero Problem

Within hours, Maria's rescue was on three news stations. The department faced a crisis: their firefighter was being called a hero for ignoring their procedures.

This created what bureaucrats call "the competence problem"—when doing the right thing makes the system look wrong.

This image shows "the competence problem" in action. How can an organization prevent this problem by ensuring that its employees are just competent enough to avoid being a "hero" but not competent enough to make the system look bad?

Chapter 18: The Phone Call That Changed Everything

City Council member Patricia Williams called with dangerous questions: *"Why do our procedures prevent firefighters from doing their jobs?"*

Chief Thompson felt his carefully constructed system of managed mediocrity beginning to wobble.

Chief Thompson's "managed mediocrity" is beginning to "wobble". What is the most effective way to respond to a "managed mediocrity" crisis?

How can you strategically give the appearance of working hard while actually doing nothing at all?

Chapter 19: The Chain Reaction

"Information flows up the chain, but decisions flow down. By the time they reach us, they make no sense," Jake explained, drawing stick figures connected by broken telephone lines.

The chain of command had become the chain that binds—protecting the organization from its own purpose.

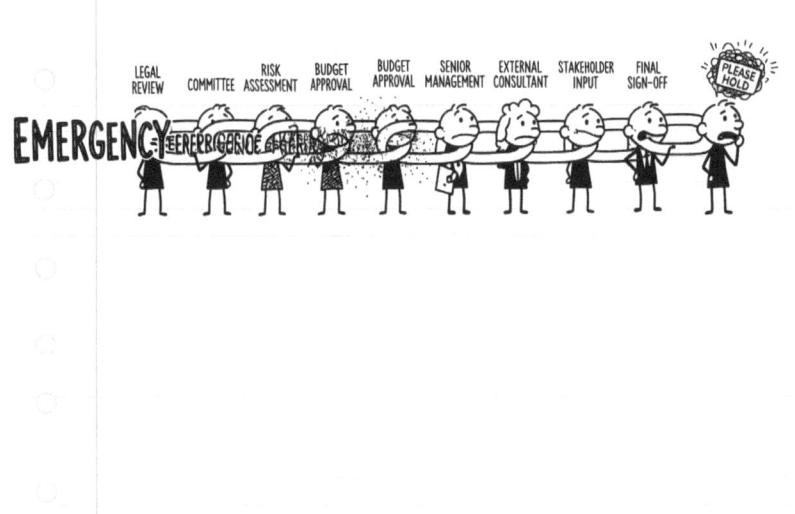

Jake explains that the chain of command has become the "chain that binds—protecting the organization from its own purpose". What are the three most effective ways to turn a simple process into a binding chain of pointless committees?

Who holds the "Please Hold" sign in your organization, and what is their primary function?

Chapter 20: The Invention of New Problems

Every solution created three new committees. The "Community Outreach Effectiveness Review Board" was formed to study why community outreach was ineffective, thus ensuring it would remain ineffective indefinitely.

Bureaucracy's greatest achievement: self-perpetuating uselessness.

The book states that "bureaucracy's greatest achievement" is "self-perpetuating uselessness". Invent a new "Problem Solver" machine that will take one solution and spit out three new committees to ensure nothing ever gets done.

Why is it more effective to study why something is ineffective rather than simply making it effective?

Chapter 21: The Meeting About the Meeting About Meetings

Chief Thompson called a meeting to discuss the unauthorized meeting where people had drawn pictures. The irony was lost on him, but not on anyone else.

"We need to establish protocols for unauthorized discussions of protocols," he announced without a trace of self-awareness.

What is the ideal number of meetings about meetings to ensure that no one ever questions why they're having the original meetings in the first place?

Chapter 22: The Awakening

The whiteboard sessions evolved from complaints to solutions. Firefighters started sketching what the department could look like if it actually focused on its mission.

"What if response protocols were written by people who actually respond?" someone suggested. Revolutionary thinking.

One character says, "Change is scary," and another says, "That's not how we've always done it". What are the psychological benefits of using these two phrases to avoid any and all progress?

Draft a memo explaining why "revolutionary thinking" is a dangerous and unacceptable violation of departmental norms.

Chapter 23: The Threat Assessment

"Captain Martinez, you have forty-eight hours to get your people back in line," Thompson warned. *"No more drawing sessions. No more questioning."*

The greatest threat to organizational dysfunction is organizational function.

The book says, "The greatest threat to organizational dysfunction is organizational function". What is the most effective way for a dysfunctional organization to protect itself from its own purpose?

You are Chief Thompson. Draft a "compliance deadline" memo that uses overly aggressive language to prevent your staff from doing their job effectively.

Chapter 24: The Two Realities

Chief Thompson's report: "Exemplary 8-minute response time. Zero casualties. Peak efficiency."

Sarah's reality: 12-minute response through broken GPS to an under-resourced neighborhood, with equipment held together by duct tape and hope.

Same incident. Different universes.

The image shows two realities for the "same incident". How can a bureaucracy create an alternate reality that serves its own needs, and how can they prevent their employees from exposing this alternate reality?

Chapter 25: The Resistance Network

Chief Thompson didn't go quietly. He formed the "Standards and Safety Coalition" with like-minded administrators from other departments.

"If we let one group ignore procedures," he warned the mayor, "soon everyone will want to 'innovate.' Where does it end?"

Assistant Chief Martinez (the other one) nodded. "Chaos. Pure chaos."

They genuinely believed that rigid systems prevented disaster. They'd never seen how rigid systems create different disasters.

You are Chief Thompson. Draft a mission statement for the "Standards and Safety Coalition" that warns of the dangers of "innovation" and "competence".

Is it possible for a group of like-minded bureaucrats to create chaos by trying to prevent it?

The Standards and Safety Coalition's Guide to Un-Learning Common Sense

1. Maria's decision to save a life by ignoring protocol is labeled a "Hero Problem." What does this title reveal about the department's values?

2. How do Chief Thompson and the "Standards and Safety Coalition" attempt to contain the "threat" of competence?

3. What are the unintended consequences of the department's effort to create a "safe" and "compliant" environment?

4. Discuss the irony in a system that fears the very competence it relies on to function.

5. How does the concept of a "hero" shift from being a positive attribute to a problem to be solved?

6. Where does the narrative tension come from in this section—is it from the fire, the bureaucracy, or both?

7. How does the "Standards and Safety Coalition" serve as a microcosm of institutional resistance to change?

THREE

Chapter 26: The Federal Intervention

The woman with the notepad wasn't from the city. She was from somewhere with more authority and fewer patience for bureaucratic nonsense.

"Help us understand why your procedures prevent your firefighters from saving lives," she said. Simple question. Complicated answer.

A federal investigator asks a simple question: "Help us understand why your procedures prevent your firefighters from saving lives". How would you, as Chief Thompson, provide a "complicated answer" without actually answering the question?

The chief is on fire in this image, but it's a bureaucratic fire. Is there a way for a bureaucrat to put out their own fire with more paperwork?

Chapter 27: The Choice

"We have good people trapped in a bad system," Sarah told the council. *"When good people can't do good work, everyone suffers."*

The room faced a choice: protect the system or protect the mission. For once, the right choice was obvious.

The room faces a choice: "protect the system" or "protect the mission". What are the key benefits of protecting a system, even when it is actively failing its mission?

Is it possible to find a third road that allows you to protect the system and the mission, so long as you do it very, very slowly?

Chapter 28: The New Fire Chief Wanted Ad

"WANTED: Fire Chief. Must understand that the best chain of command connects people to purpose, not separates them from it. Actual firefighting experience preferred but not required if you can spell 'mission' correctly."

Change was coming, one burnt procedure at a time.

The new wanted ad for a Fire Chief states that a candidate "must understand that the best chain of command connects people to purpose, not separates them from it". How can we translate this from bureaucratic language into a resume bullet point?

Chapter 29: The Fire That Lights the Way

The most dangerous fires aren't always in burning buildings. Sometimes they're the flames that burn away bureaucratic barriers, lighting the path toward organizations that actually work.

Sarah and Maria walked back to the station, two firefighters who'd learned that the most important fires to tend are the ones that illuminate new possibilities.

The book states that the "most dangerous fires aren't always in burning buildings" but are the ones that burn "bureaucratic barriers". When is it appropriate to commit arson on a pile of useless paperwork and/or processes?

You have just started a new job in a bureaucratic organization. Write a list of the top ten "useless procedures" you will attempt to burn down, even if it gets you in the "hot seat?"

Chapter 30: The Pilot Program

"Six months," Sarah announced to her crew. "City Council approved a pilot program. We design our own response protocols for District 7."

The catch? Everything had to be measured, documented, and compared to the old system.

"No pressure," Maria laughed. "Just prove that competence works better than compliance."

They had six months to show that connecting people to purpose beats protecting people from responsibility.

The pilot program's catch is that everything must be "measured, documented, and compared to the old system". What are the 2-3 most important metrics to include in a pilot program that is designed to fail?

Chapter 31: The Success Metrics

Three months into the pilot:

District 7 response times: Down 40% Community complaints: Down 60% Equipment downtime: Down 30% Firefighter satisfaction: Up 70% Chief Thompson's blood pressure: Up 50%

"The numbers don't tell the whole story," he insisted to anyone who would listen.

He was right. The numbers didn't show Mrs. Rodriguez's grandson timing their response at 3 minutes, 47 seconds.

Chief Thompson claims that the numbers "don't tell the whole story," and he is right. What are the three most important unmeasured metrics in an organization, and how can you use these metrics to prove that the organization is a complete failure?

Write a memo from Chief Thompson to his superiors, explaining why a 40% reduction in response time and a 70% increase in firefighter satisfaction are actually "dangerous" and "unacceptable".

Chapter 32: The Implementation Challenge

Success created new problems. Other districts wanted the same flexibility. The mayor wanted to expand the program citywide.

But Deputy Chief Wilson raised the obvious question: "How do we maintain standards when everyone's doing something different?"

This was the real challenge: scaling good judgment instead of just scaling procedures.

Sarah's answer: "Maybe standards should be about outcomes, not methods."

Revolutionary thinking in a world built on process compliance.

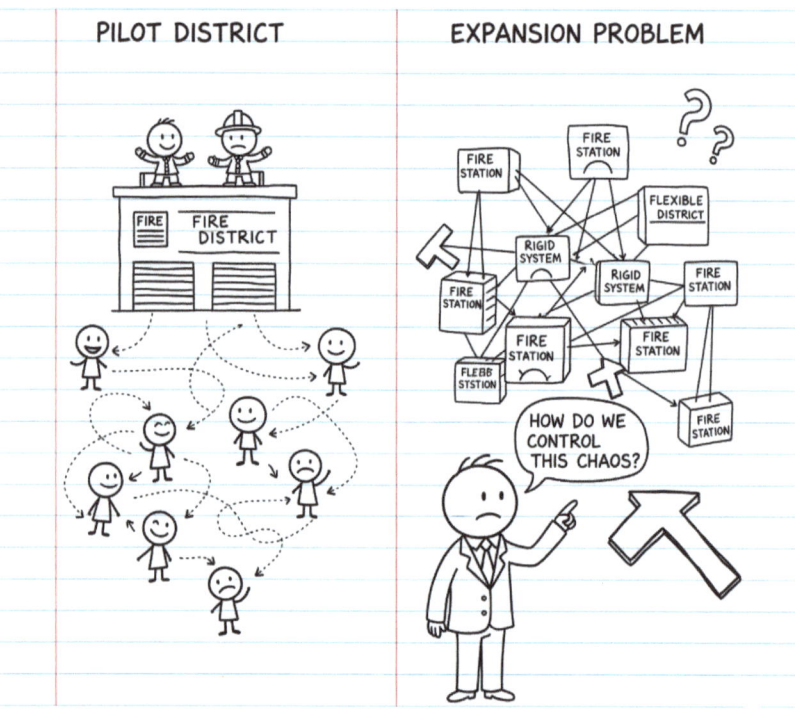

What is the most effective way to "control this chaos" of good judgment, and why is it important to control it in the first place?

Chapter 33: The Mentor System

The solution came from an unexpected source: the firefighters themselves.

"Pair experienced crews with new ones," Maria suggested. "Not for supervision—for teaching. Show them what works, let them figure out how."

It was ancient wisdom: apprenticeship. Learning by doing with guidance, not by memorizing rules without context.

Within weeks, knowledge was flowing faster than it had in years. People were teaching each other instead of waiting to be taught.

The changes didn't stay in District 7. How does the "viral" spread of positive change compare to the slow, "burning" effect of bureaucracy that was seen in Act One?

Given the examples of the police, schools, and library, what is the most significant challenge in ensuring this positive change becomes the new norm across an entire city?

Chapter 34: The New Normal

Six months later, the pilot program wasn't a pilot anymore. It was just how District 7 worked.

Chief Thompson had been reassigned to "Strategic Planning" (a bureaucratic euphemism for "office with no responsibilities"). His replacement was Captain Martinez, promoted after the fastest confirmation hearing in city history.

The new chief's first policy change: "Use your judgment. We'll figure out the paperwork later."

Maria now times how fast "good ideas spread". Create a new metric for measuring the spread of a good idea, and include a section on how you will use this metric to prevent the spread of bad ideas.

Chapter 35: The Fire That Spreads

The changes didn't stay in District 7. Police started asking why they needed seventeen signatures for overtime. Schools questioned why field trips required six-month advance approval. The library wondered why purchasing a $12 book took the same process as buying a $12,000 computer.

Sometimes the most important fire you fight isn't in a building. It's the one that burns through institutional barriers, lighting the way toward organizations that remember why they exist.

Maria still carries a stopwatch. But now she times how fast good ideas spread, not how long bad procedures take.

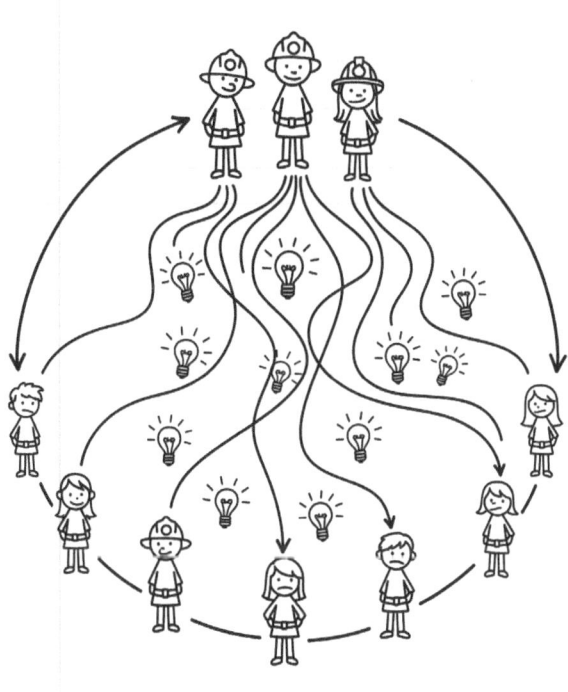

The chapter shows that a good idea, once implemented, can spread like a contagion. When a positive change goes viral in an organization, what are the biggest challenges it faces? What is the institutional equivalent of an "immune system" that tries to reject it?

Epilogue Box

"Sometimes the most dangerous fires are the ones that burn slowly, consuming purpose one procedure at a time. But sometimes, if you're lucky, those same fires can light the way to something better."

The Fire Within: When bureaucracy meets its match, everyone wins except the bureaucrats.

VIRAL COMPETENCE

Maria's stopwatch used to measure delays and incompetence—the time it took to get approval for a hose, the minutes lost to a broken GPS. Now, she timed something new: the spread of a good idea. Her stopwatch clicked as the police department adopted a more efficient overtime process and the school district streamlined its field trip approvals. Each tick was a small victory, a new domino falling in a chain reaction of common sense. The old system, the "chain that binds," was now being replaced by a network of people connected by a shared purpose.

Reflective Question:

What institutional immune systems exist to prevent the spread of good ideas, and how do we bypass them?

Chief Thompson had been reassigned to "Strategic Planning," a well-known bureaucratic euphemism for being sent to a room with no responsibilities. From his new office, he watched as his former department flourished under Captain Martinez's leadership. The new chief's first policy—"Use your judgment. We'll figure out the paperwork later"—was a direct reversal of everything he had built. The numbers—reduced response times, increased satisfaction—were undeniable, yet he insisted they didn't tell the "whole story". He was right; they didn't show the bureaucratic fire that had been extinguished and the new one that was now lighting the way.

Reflective Question:

What happens when a system is so invested in its own dysfunction that it considers success a failure?

The department, fueled by its newfound efficiency, went to the polls. They had a new leader in mind, someone who promised to "fix" the system by "getting rid of all the rules." Mayor O'Malley was a charismatic firebrand, elected on a platform of pure chaos. She dismantled the department's new, effective protocols, arguing that a system of "good judgment" was a slippery slope to anarchy. Her every decision was a performance, a grand gesture of defiance against the very notion of common sense. She would declare victory over a minor procedural win while ignoring the major fires burning across the city. The department's firefighters, once heroes in a battle against bureaucracy, now found themselves fighting a new kind of slow-burning fire—a political one, fanned by the very person they had elected to lead.

Reflective Question:

What happens when the people's desire to dismantle bureaucracy leads them to elect a system that is even more dysfunctional?

The fire station was a point of pride, a symbol of community resilience. It sat at the heart of the neighborhood, and its doors were always open. The firefighters, known for their quick response to medical emergencies, their community outreach, and their willingness to help with everything from clearing a fallen tree to helping a senior citizen with their groceries, were as much a part of the community as the local library or the corner store. But a new leader, a "community organizer" who had never spent a day in the neighborhood, began to spread a different narrative. She saw the station not as a resource but as a nuisance, a symbol of "dependency" and "unearned privilege." Ignoring the data, the community testimonials, and the pleas of local residents, she began a campaign to have the fire station relocated. She claimed she was "protecting the community," when in reality, she was creating a new kind of fire—a blaze of misinformation and division—that threatened to burn down the very sense of community the fire station had helped build.

Reflective Question:

How does the spread of misinformation fan the flames of division and destroy the very things a community has worked so hard to build?

The fires that consume purpose aren't extinguished by luck; they're extinguished by people. You can call them institutional barriers, micromanagement, or organizational silos, but at the end of the day, it's just a name for a story we've been told—a story that says we're powerless to change things. The real fire, the one that makes a difference, is the one you decide to light. It doesn't matter how big or small the bureaucracy is, because the moment you choose to act—the moment you challenge a single procedure or trust a person to use their judgment—you become the spark. This book is a story about a team that chose to act. Now, it's a story about you.

www.ingramcontent.com/pod-product-compliance
Lightning Source LLC
Chambersburg PA
CBHW042217050426
42453CB00001BA/4